Peace Poems

Created to Promote Peace

Amani Nigia Williams

Tallahassee, FL

Copyright © January 2016
By Amani Nigia Williams

All rights reserved. No part of this book may be reproduced in any form without the expressed written permission of the publisher, except by a reviewer.

Printed by CreateSpace for:

Amani Publishing, LLC
P. O. Box 12045
Tallahassee, FL 32317
(850) 264-3341

A company based on faith, hope, and love

ISBN: 9781523444359

LCCN: 2016902376

Visit our website at: www.barbarajoe.webs.com

Email us at: amanipublishing@aol.com

Author's photograph by: Stan Johnson
Cover photograph courtesy of: www.bigstock.com
Cover designed by: Adrienne Thompson

Introduction

Welcome to my book of peace poems. I hope that while you're reading these poems, you will be inspired to write and be part of a cause. The cause that I'm talking about is to spread peace.

I would like you to tell your family and friends about my book.

~Love, Amani

Acknowledgements

I acknowledge Jesus as my Savior. I want to thank Him for giving me the inspiration and the talent to write this book.

I acknowledge my parents for encouraging me to keep going and to finish my poetry book.

I acknowledge Pace Center for Girls for helping me speak out, even if it is on paper.

I acknowledge Mrs. Felicia Thomas for editing my book and giving me positive feedback.

I also acknowledge the Tallahassee Authors Network members for their overall encouragement.

Dedication

I dedicate this book to all my family and friends who have supported me through this journey.

I also dedicate this book to the Leon County Public Library for supporting teen poets.

Table of Contents

Part One 10
Peace 11
Black Lives Matter 12
I'm Black and I'm Proud 13
I'm Proud of Myself 15
What is Love? 16
My Greatest Fear 17
R-E-S-P-E-C-T 18
Happiness Everyday 19
Veteran's Day 20
Who Am I? 22
Birthday 24
Bird 26
On Mother's Day 27
CHRISTMAS 28
Love Is 29
Why Do You Hate Me? 30
War 31
Love 32
My Next Life 33
Do You Hear the People? 34
Telling Me Lies 35
Don't Judge Me 36
Pain 37

Am I dreaming?	38
Can You See Me?	39
I Don't Know	40
Save My Soul	41
Good Morning	42
Goodbye	43
Pace Center for Girls	44
Roses	45
Memories	46
Time	47
You Don't Care About Me	48
Why Judge People?	49
Is It Worth It?	50
I'm Ready to Go	51
Where Can I Lay?	52
Part 2	54
An Ode to My Mother	55
An Ode to Someone Who is Mad	56
Cali, My Special Dog	57
Meg	58
Bubbles	59
Seasons	60
Candy	61
An Elegy to Sunny	62
Jingle Bells	63

Ice cream 64
Jumping Monkey 65
Christmas 66
Winter 67
Thank You Message from Amani: 68
About the Author 69

PeaceArtSite.com

Peace art created to share with the hope for peace!

Part One

Teen Poems

Peace

A peaceful world

That's all I want

That's all I see

No more killing

No more fights

Enough is enough

We need to try

To do better

To be better

And to love one another

World peace is all I want.

Black Lives Matter

Our lives matter
Because we are all the same
It shouldn't matter
If we come from the South or North
All that matters
Is our personality and what we can do

It shouldn't matter
If we pay for food with an EBT card
Or a black card
We are all still eating the same food

It shouldn't matter that
I have long, black dreads
I am not a criminal
You look at my appearance and
Already think you know
My whole life story
Well, news flash, you don't
Just like you, we have dreams, too
Like becoming a doctor
Or the President of the United States
We are important and we will fight
For our rights
Our skin color doesn't define us
We do.

I'm Black and I'm Proud

I'm black and I'm proud

People try to bring me down
Because of my skin color
But my skin color
Doesn't define who I am

I am proud that
I am a young black woman
Because if I weren't
I wouldn't understand the suffering
Of my ancestors and what they had
To do to survive

I'm black and I'm proud
Of my long black dreadlocks
My hair makes me who I am
It makes me different
A good different

I'm black and I'm proud
That my parents taught me everything
I need to know
So I won't go into this world
Expecting life to be easy for me

I'm black and I'm proud
That we are making a difference
In this world
To the first black doctor
To the first black president

I'm black and I'm proud to say
That I will not judge you
For your skin color,
Religion,
Background,
Or sexuality

All I ask for is respect
Like I have for you
Because I'm black
And I'm proud.

I'm Proud of Myself

I'm proud of myself
I could be anything I want
But if it weren't for myself
Doing it without any help
Then I wouldn't be proud
I would just be getting by
Who wants to just barely get by?
When you could have been so much more

I'm proud of my achievements
That makes me stronger each and every day
Sometimes, you may not be proud
Of your mistakes
But if you never make a mistake
You can never learn from it
And become a better person
I'm proud that I go to church every Sunday
To learn the way of the Lord, my Savior

I'm proud of the way I'm treating myself
To become a strong, independent,
Black woman
I'm proud of the life I'm living
Which has love, peace, and happiness
And lastly,
I'm just proud of myself.

What is Love?

Love is when someone loves you for you
Love is when you can stay together
Through the trials and tribulations
To love someone is like finding your better half
Someone that you can move forward with
Who won't judge you for your mistakes

Love is something you feel in your heart
You cannot buy love, it's hard to come by
But when you find that person,
Don't let them go
Love is caring about how your day went
And your mind set

Love is everlasting
Just like the Bible says,
"God so loved the world that He gave us
His only begotten son."
That has to be very hard
To let someone you love to pieces go
But love is strong and powerful

Love is like a river
It can go steady at times and others,
It becomes rapid, but this is
What love is…
Love never ends.

My Greatest Fear

My greatest fear is what will happen
After I'm dead
What if I go to heaven or hell?
What if I stay on earth?
I fear that the world will be different
After I'm dead

Like it could be bad and my children
Will have to be in it
I fear the afterlife because I don't
Know what's going to happen
That can be good or bad
It's almost like trying something different

I know what the Bible says,
That I can have everlasting life
But what if I mess up and do something bad
Will I still have everlasting life?
Or will I go down and be with the devil?
Or it could be something that I can escape
So I would be a fallen angel
Not ready to leave this earth

I'm not scared to die
If the Lord takes me
He can have me
But I fear the afterlife.

R-E-S-P-E-C-T

(Dedicated to Auntie Nella)

The person that I respect a lot is
My Auntie Nella

I respect her because she inspires me
To be in the Lord and learn
The ways to success
She is a pastor and I go to her church
Every Sunday and sometimes on Wednesdays

I feel like we share the same traits
She is like my other mother
She takes me places like the mall to shop
Or sometimes we go to the hospital
And talk to the patients
And pray with them
I really respect her for going with
Her heart and soul
And following the ways of the Lord

I can talk to her about any
And everything
And she will give me advice
I'm really happy
That she is in my life.

Happiness Everyday

I experience happiness everyday
I don't let a lot of thing get to me
I try to think of the positive things in life
To me, there is no reason for people
To be unhappy over the little things in life
There are always going to be good and bad days
But you have to be in a positive state of mind

The things that make me extremely happy are
My fish, Jelly, and
My dog, Cali
They mean the world to me

I'm normally nice to everyone
Even if some people don't like them
But if they prove to be
Who they say they are not
I have to question myself
And see if I wanna be in an
Unhealthy relationship with them still

To be happy is such a wonderful thing
Because you can go into life
With a positive attitude
People will love to be around you
And be your friend.

Veteran's Day

I like to celebrate Veteran's Day
Because of what veterans
Had to go through
And what they learned

My Mom and Dad
Were both in the military
My Mom was in the Navy
Working with computers
And my Dad was in the Marines

My Dad always talks about
His experience in the Marines
He talks about how
They had to dress
Where they went like,
Greece and Italy
He also says that
They would play pranks on people,
Like putting their beds outside
Or in the water

My Mom and Dad
Met in the military
And got married
My uncles were in the Army, too
I'm just happy that

They didn't get injured,
Died, or have mental problems
They have fought
For my freedom
And where I am today

Other families have
Gone through a lot
Some have died,
Killed themselves
Had mental problems,
Or lost body parts

It's really sad to think
About all the people
Who died in war
And cannot be found
Or recognized.

Who Am I?

Who am I, really … hmm?

I know who I am
I am Amani Nigia Williams
A confident, independent, strong,
And powerful person
I can do anything that I put my mind to
I'm still a little quiet, calm, and collected

I am adopted but I don't let that control
My future
I have a lot of accomplishments that
I am proud of like, Soccer,
Track, and African dance

I am going to do bigger and better things
My grades have changed since my old school
A's and B's now
I am not afraid if people will not
Appreciate the real me

I don't care what other people
Think or feel about me
I am the only one who knows
The real me
Nobody can tell me who I am

I am very adventurous and courageous
I have a strong mind
I can keep my cool
When something is wrong, because
I know who I am

I play the piano, guitar, and drums
So that I have something to do
At all times
I am a bookworm
I love reading books
Especially fantasy and mystery

Every Monday, Wednesday, Thursday,
And Saturday
I go to the gym and exercise
I love myself and that's all that matters
I am peaceful, happy, and always smiling
I may laugh a lot, but I know
When it's the appropriate time

I am just me.

Birthday

Happy Birthday!
You're getting older now
You're taller
Your clothes fit you different now
Birthdays are a big celebration
You have a party
Invite a couple of friends
You dance
Talk
And just have fun
Opening tons of presents
From everyone
From gift cards
To shoes

Oh, the best part is coming up
The big birthday cake
Everyone gathers around
And sings Happy Birthday
Then you make a wish
And with a big blow
You blow out the candles
Parents give you the first big piece
And serve everyone else a piece
The cake is so delicious
With tasty frosting and sprinkles

The saddest part is leaving
You say, "Thank you"
And hand out goody bags to go
This is the end of the party
Now it's time to go home

Home at last
Home at last
Thank God Almighty
That we're home at last.

Bird

I wanna be a bird
So I can fly high
And soar into the sky
I wanna have large colorful wings
And spread my wings out wide
I want to fly above the trees
So I can look down
And see what people are doing
To see how it
Feels to glide
I can eat off the feeders
And bathe in the fountains
Migrate when it starts
To get a little cold

Oh, but I have to watch out
Other animals may try
To get me
And eat me
I can sit in a tree
And just sing
Watching the squirrels play
Up and down the tree
I wanna be a bird.

On Mother's Day

I just want to say, "Happy Mother's Day."

Mom, today is your day
To relax and enjoy yourself
A day to celebrate
And be thankful for you
You have taken care of me for 15 years
Even though we have our ups and downs,
You are still there for me
You mean the world to me
I really appreciate you
Even though I don't say it,
You are the best mom
I could ask for
I am thankful to be able
To call you my mom

Happy Mother's Day
I love you!

You're such a terrific friend!

Love, Amani

CHRISTMAS

Christmas is the season for celebration

Happy thoughts all around,
Hope you come home on time

Ringing of the jingle bells
Makes a sound up and down

Ice covering the ground and big snow clouds

Sleds going down the hill, laughing is all I hear

Togetherness is what this season is all about

Mistletoe hanging from the ceiling
Waiting for a kiss

Artificial tree in the living room
With all the gifts under it

Santa is coming down the chimney

It's Christmas.

Love Is

Love is powerful
Love will never fall down
Love can be hard

Love is a contagious word
Love is sweet
Love is grand

Love is a magical thing
Love is what helps you through
Love is everything

Love is a red rose
That shines so bright
You cannot see it

I love me and
Everyone in the world

Love never dies.

Why Do You Hate Me?

Why do you hate me?

Do you hate me because of my skin?

Or the knowledge I have

Knowledge that intimidates you?

Do you hate me because of my hair?

Hair that is nappy and curly

Do you hate me because of the way I dress?

Dress like I have places to be

And people to see

Why do you hate me?

War

Today, war is the only thing we know

We kill for a hobby

Fights that our own people cause

Are we alive?

Because when I go to sleep

I see darkness

But when I wake up

I see death all over the news and paper

Would you rather live in darkness?

Or see the death of millions each day?

Love

Love

That's one powerful word

Everybody wants love

Animals, humans,

And even insects

Loving someone is being

Able to look past

All of their differences

To respect each other is

Love.

My Next Life

What will I be

In my next life?

Will I be a bird?

That flies to new heights

Will I be a dog?

That protects people

Will I be a lion?

That hunts prey

What will I be?

Will I be a fish?

That swims in the ocean

In my next life.

Do You Hear the People?

Do you hear the people?

People that sing songs
People who write books

Do you hear the people?

People who are dying
Because of the color of their skin

The kids that are suffering

The homeless people that
Live on the street

Can you hear?
The gun shots
The killing

Can you hear them?

Do you hear the people?

Telling Me Lies

You're always telling me lies

Lies that are too fake to believe

Lies that I can't understand

Why lie?

The truth always come to light.

To be continued...

Don't Judge Me

Don't judge me

Because of the way I act

Don't call me a hood rat.

To be continued...

Pain

Everyone copes with pain

In a different way

Some cry like there is no tomorrow

Some scream so loud that glass breaks

Pain makes people do crazy things

Some drink the pain away

Some smoke to get high

Some pain is unbearable.

Am I dreaming?

Am I a baby who is asleep

But dreaming?

Dreaming of when I get older

When I go to sleep

And dream

Am I awake in another life?

Dreaming about the real life

Where people are dying

And some are crying?

Am I dreaming?

Can You See Me?

Can you see me?

I'm standing alone

Can you hear me?

I'm singing a song

I am happy to be alone

Can you feel me?

I'm hugging you all

Are we friends or foul?

Can you love me?

With all my flaws

Can you see me?

I Don't Know

I don't know
But I feel free
Free from everything
Things that hurt me

I can sing a song
To hide the pain
I am stronger than you
But I cry

You call me weak
And I listen to what you say
I'm a kind person who
Smiles and laughs
With everyone

But some people
Will never understand me
And I can't change their minds
Because I don't know how.

Save My Soul

Save my soul, Lord
Make me stronger than yesterday
Hear me, Lord
I'm not a little girl anymore
I've grown up
I now know the meaning of your love
Lord, I may make mistakes
But I'm trying to do better
I'm praying to you today
Because I need you right now
I want to praise you, Lord
Harder than before
Can you help me now?

Save my soul, Lord
Make me wiser
Wiser than yesterday
I need to think about what I have done
I need knowledge of you, Lord
I want to sing to you
Louder than before
I don't want to be scared anymore
Because, Lord, I believe in you
Believe that you will help me
Through all of the tough times
Please, save my soul.

Good Morning

Good morning
I have woken up today
Happy as ever

If I'm awake
That means I didn't die
The Lord has woken
Me up another day
It was not my time to go
So I get to have another day

The birds are chirping
And the bugs are flying
The grass is greener
Flowers are brighter

The sun is shining
The wind is blowing
Animals are playing

The water is flowing
It smells wonderful outside
Warm and cozy

Good Morning.

Goodbye

It is my time to say goodbye
I'm leaving this world
Hopefully,
I helped change it
Made it a better place

I have done everything I could
From helping people
To animals
And with the work I've done
I know that I've changed
People's lives around me
From walking my dog, Cali
To volunteering at
Kids Incorporated

You will see me again
In another life
Where I will be stronger
And powerful
My mind will be wiser
Beyond my years

Good-bye old world

And Hello new world.

Pace Center for Girls

Pace is a place where girls can learn
All Pace girls have stories
We are all different
We all have different backgrounds
But we are all one
I feel like I've known these girls
My whole life
Like sisters, we stick together
But every now and then, we do fight
Even though we fight, we are still sisters
We can tell each other stuff
We normally don't say
Because we trust each other
Trust is a big word
But at Pace, we do use it
We work at our own pace
To get our grades right

At Pace, there is a variety of girls
There are black, white, mixed, Hispanic,
And all types
We laugh together, sing together
Do spoken word together
I feel loved at Pace by all the girls
Thank you for giving me these experiences

I am proud to be a Pace girl.

Roses

People say roses are red

But they can be all types of colors

Roses smell good when

You first get them

But when they start dying

They start to stink

That's just like life

One minute life is all good

But when something bad happens

Life starts to stink.

Memories

Some memories are good
Some show the bad
It's so bad,
You can't function anymore
You get nightmares about them
But some of the good ones
Could be your birthday
Christmas, Easter,
Or even just going to the park

A lot of memories hold pain
Pain that is powerful
The painful memories can
Cause depression
The pain of someone close to you
Dies or your pet

I have happy memories
Where I laugh at them sometimes
Like when I fell at Wild Adventures
I love to smile at the good memories
Like when I got my dog
The painful memories are tough
Like when my favorite cousin died.
I still remember him like it was yesterday.
Playing with him is my best memory.

Time

There is time
Time will never last forever
Everyone's time will run out
So we shouldn't take it for granted
We should travel places
That haven't been discovered
People say we have
All the time in the world
But that is not true
Because when we die
There is no more time
For us

So we should become
Something that will change the nation
We never know how much time we have
So use it wisely
You have time to help
Someone in need
Help the poor
Because their time is slowly ending
They don't have as many opportunities
As we do
We need to give our time
To be important
And help others in need.

You Don't Care About Me

You don't care about me
Because I am black

If I get shot by someone
That person wouldn't go to jail

Why?
Because of my color

Why don't you care?
Is it because I'm too tall
For the average girl?

Can it be because of my dreads?
That make me look like
I've done something

Why don't you care?
Is it because I wear
A hoodie around?

Do I intimidate you with my hands?
That make me look like I can fight?

Why don't you care about me?

Why Judge People?

Why do you judge people?
Is it for fun?
You don't even know their story
What is the point?
Is it to put people down?
To make them cry
To hurt them

Why do you judge people?
To make them kill themselves
So now you feel guilty
Wishing that you could take it all back
But it's too late
You're going to have to live
With knowing that you are the reason
Why they took their life
You shouldn't have made fun of them
Not knowing that
They can't afford new clothes
So they wear the same clothes
Over and over again
You don't know that their parents
Who are supposed to take care
And love them
Are abusing and hurting them
And you just added on to more pain
Why judge people?

Is It Worth It?

Is it worth it?
Is all this pain worth it?
Pain of killing someone
Is all the killing worth it?
Killing people for money
Or just for the fun of it
Is it worth killing
Nine black people in church?
Do you not have any respect at all?
Do you not care that
You're going to jail to suffer?
But is it worth it?
Worth the death
Death of millions

Is it worth it?
All the equal rights
But we are not free
From the hate,
Cruelty, and killings
It is like we are already dead
Because how can we live
In this hateful world?
Where is the peace, the love,
And the happiness?
Is it worth it?

I'm Ready to Go

I'm ready to go
Go to a place
Where there is
Happiness, joy
And laughter
Where I can be myself
Without anyone judging me
I'm ready to go
To a place
Where there is water
Sandcastles, and seashells
Where I can play in the sand
Without looking childish

I'm ready to go
To a place
Where I can learn
Learn about Math
Science, English, and History
Where there are teachers
I can ask for help
Without people laughing at me
If my question is stupid
But I just can't grasp the subject

I'm ready to go.

Where Can I Lay?

Where can I lay?

Can I lay on a bed?

With a warm blanket
To keep me warm

Can I lay on a couch?

With a fluffy pillow
So my neck won't hurt

Can I lay on the floor?

With socks on my feet
To keep my feet hot

Can I lay in a car?

With the heater on
Because it is cold

Can I lay on the sidewalk?

With a dog
So I won't be alone

Can I lay under a bridge?

With a jacket
So I can stay dry

Can I lay in the park?

With a backpack
So I can sit on it.

Where can I lay?

Part 2

Pre-teen Poems

PLAY NICE

TEACH PEACE

An Ode to My Mother

You make me laugh
I love you so much

You take me out to eat
Buy me new clothes

What else could a girl ask for?
Except for love

We play the Wii,
I beat you all the time
But you can't hate the player
Hate the game

We watch TV together
And eat popcorn
Your favorite show is CSI: Miami
I love to watch that show with you

All I want to say is that

I love you.

An Ode to Someone Who is Mad

I made you mad once
I say sorry, you won't forgive me

The next day you punch me
But I guess I needed that

Just leave me on the side of the curb
I will still be there waiting

Where you left me crying
I go north to catch the fastest train

I left you a note but don't read it
Just do what you did to the last one

Like you care about my feelings
Could not say it to my face

I'm free from my past
And a new day is coming.

Cali, My Special Dog

Have you ever gotten something special
That you did not pay for?

Yes, I have.

I got a yellow Labrador retriever
That is named Cali
AKA "my little coconut head"

I have always wanted a dog
That was special to me

She inspires me when I am feeling down
Because she is always happy to see me

I always wanted a dog
But I did not have any money to buy one
Then, I asked Santa six years ago

To bring me a dog, a
And I got a little coconut head
On Christmas morning.

She is very special to me.

Meg

Meg o Meg

You smell sour

How can you stand flour?

I see your fear

As your last tear

That fear you have is power.

Bubbles

Bubbles

You blow bubbles

They float away

Bubbles fly so high

Bubbles will not return

Float up,

Up and away

The sad part is

Bubbles pop

And that is the end of bubbles.

Seasons

Spring

Warm

Cozy

Refreshing, relaxing

Uplifting

Cool

Enjoyable

Heat

Muggy,

Scorching, sizzling,

Searing,

Hot, miserable

Summer

Candy

C is for cookies

A is for apple

N is for now and later

D is for donut

Y is for yogurt

An Elegy to Sunny

Sunny O Sunny
My loveable hamster

Your eyes sparkled like stars in the sky
You ate like a pig
But I loved you anyway

I miss your wheel turning every night
You were the only one I could talk to
Sunny, my love,
I wish you were here so I could tell you
What's going on here

I will always love you
I know you can hear me
Talking to you everyday
I think of you everyday

I miss you dearly,
Sunny Williams
I will see you again and
We can go back to
Eating carrots together

Bye, Sunny.

Jingle Bells

J is for jingle
I is for ice cream
N is for nutmeg
G is for goodness
L is for laughter
E is for enjoy

B is for bells
E is for eggs
L is for life
L is for love
S is for spirit

Ice cream

Ice cream
Ice cream

Mango ice cream
Mint ice cream
Brownie batter
Yummy ice cream
Cotton candy sweet ice cream

Those are just a few
Rainbow ice cream
Chocolate ice cream
Vanilla bean rocket ice cream

Chocolate chip chunks ice cream
Pineapple ice cream
Cookies and cream ice cream
Pecan ice cream

Don't forget rocky mountain ice cream

Last of all, but best of all

I like cookie dough ice cream.

Jumping Monkey

There once was a jumping monkey

And jumping he would always be

He fell off a cliff

Because he was stiff

Now jumping he will never be.

Christmas

C is for Christ

H is for holiday

R is for Rudolph

I is for icicle

S is for snow

T is for trees

M is for Mary who bore a son

A is for antler

S is for Santa

Winter

W is for wonderful

I is for icy

N is for noel

T is for trees

E is for everlasting love

R is for reindeer

Thank You Message from Amani

Thank you, everyone, for buying my *Peace Poems* book. I hope that I have inspired you to spread the word about peace.

This book is not just for me, but it is for you, so that you can start writing your own poems about peace.

Thank you, again. If you would like to contact me or send me a poem, my email address is: Amani_96@ymail.com

About the Author

Amani Nigia Williams is a teenager enrolled in high school in Tallahassee, Florida. She lives at home with both her parents, who are very proud of her achievements. When she graduates from high school, Amani plans to enroll in college to pursue her dreams of becoming a chef and a veterinarian. One day, she plans to open an animal adoption shelter so that all homeless animals will have homes and good food to eat.

Amani is an active member of Life Eternal Ministries where she sings in the choir and is a new member of the Usher Board. When she's not writing poetry, she enjoys reading fantasy and horror stories, watching fantasy and horror movies, listening to music, and hanging out with her friends.

Her email address is: Amani_96@ymail.com

www.peaceartsite.com